LOUDER

THAN

THUNDER

Written by Cheryl K. Hawkins

www.xulonpress.com

To Ms. Debra Adule
from Miss Cheryl Hawkins

As a fellow worker
at Compton Elementary,
I hope you enjoy this
book.

C. Hawkins

4-21-16

I would like to extend a special "thank you" to my sister, Michele Johnson, who was my chief editor and priceless consultant as I wrote this book.

In memory of my parents, Emile and Meriam Hawkins,
who have been married forty-two years and raised
five children.

Dedication

This book is dedicated to all my siblings and their family members who prayed us through this storm; to the Johnson, the Grant, the Hawkins, and the Wright families; also to the members of the body of Christ at the East-West Church in Austell, Georgia, who interceded for my father and me as we went through this ordeal. It is also dedicated to my fellow alumni from Oral Roberts University, classes of 79, 80, and 81 who remembered me and kept me in their prayers.

Acts 12:5
"...But prayer was made without ceasing of the church
unto God for (her)..."

Foreword

By Pastor Janet Mushegan Watson

I watched the news with disbelief about the accounts of devastation in the aftermath of Hurricane Katrina. However, as is often the case when hearing of events of such magnitude, there is a surreal feeling associated with the images being presented by the media. In this concise, but poignant account of one little New Orleans family's struggle for survival in the ravages of this monster storm, Cheryl provides a window into the firsthand experiences of these "victims turned victors" by abiding in the power and grace of Jesus Christ. I greatly enjoyed this book and I pray that you also will find it captivating.

LOUDER

THAN

THUNDER

Written by Cheryl K. Hawkins

Table of Contents

Introduction

This is the story of how my encounter with Hurricane Katrina has enriched my life. It is not written to be politically correct, nor is it politically motivated. It is simply a testimony of the faithfulness, mercy, and grace of God toward our family.

Romans 8: 35,37,39
Who shall separate us from the love of Christ?
Shall tribulation or distress, or persecution, or famine, or nakedness, or peril, or sword?
Yet in all these things we are more than conquerors through Him who loved us.
For I am persuaded that nothing shall be able to separate us from the love of God which is in Christ Jesus our Lord.

CHAPTER 1

Forewarned

During the month of August, I was studying the book of Esther in the bible. You remember that story don't you? As a young girl, Esther's homeland was ravaged by war and her people were taken captive. Yet she grew up, was chosen to be queen, and reigned on behalf of her people. She and her older cousin Mordecai, brought liberty to their people even in the midst of captivity!

My attention was also focused on II Kings chapters 24 & 25 and II Chronicles chapter 36. These chapters describe how the people of Judah and Jerusalem were taken captive and their nation was destroyed. Overnight, life as they knew it changed forever.

As I studied these passages a thought occurred to me. *Cheryl, what if you went to sleep one night and woke up the next morning and your life was completely different? Nothing was the same and it never will be again! What if all the places you frequently go to now suddenly became non-existent and you had no more contact with the people that you usually see everyday? How would you handle that?* I didn't take it to heart at that time. However, as I look back, I realize God was preparing me.

Friday, August 26, 2005

On Friday evening all of the news media in the metro New Orleans area was abuzz with the approaching Hurricane Katrina, a MONSTER of a storm! It was a potential five hurricane with winds up to 165 miles per hour and an eye 26 miles in diameter, the size of Lake Ponchartrain! The news media warned us, "This IS NOT the type of storm you want to ride out! Not only is this storm dangerous, but the aftermath could be worse, with a tide surge of up to 25 feet high." Yes, New Orleans was adequately forewarned!

Even the news stations and their reporters relocated outside the metro New Orleans area to cover the storm. Some news stations moved to Baton Rouge and some to Mississippi. Thus, they did their broadcasts from the new locations. They've never had to relocate before to cover a hurricane! That's how dangerous this storm was!

I walked around the house listening to the radio throughout the evening, knowing we should evacuate. I even began packing emergency needs. I tried to persuade my Daddy to leave, but he couldn't see it. Yet, I could not leave him at home alone. Why?

You see, my Daddy is a 70-year-old wheelchair bound man. One leg is 3 ½ inches shorter than the other due to a degenerative bone disease that has affected his hip. He has ebony skin, gray hair around his ears, but is bald at the top. Even in a wheelchair he has a very intimidating demeanor and at first glance anyone can tell that he is one who doesn't play!

In October 1999, my mother was diagnosed with colon cancer. I took care of her most of the following year as she battled the disease, but for some reason, she refused to follow the doctor's orders. Throughout that year it was difficult to get her to keep her doctor appointments and when she did go she wouldn't cooperate. She refused to take the treat-

20

ments that were offered to her. When we saw that she had an urgency to leave, we finally decided to release her. My parents had been married for forty-two years and three days up to the time of her passing. She died October 28, 2000 at the age of 63, and it's just been my dad and me ever since. The rest of my siblings live in Georgia with their families. I felt a responsibility to stay with Daddy and ride out the storm since it was just the two of us. God forbid that I evacuated, left him alone in the midst of the hurricane, and some misfortune happened to him. I couldn't live with that on my conscience.

Instead of my dad preparing to leave, he kept boasting, "Where is your faith? Nothing's going to happen to us. We'll be alright. We've ridden out hurricanes before and we were safe." He was right! Our family has lived in New Orleans for over 40 years and went through several hurricanes with no damage to our property. Camille, Elena, Florence, Andrew and Betsy were just a few of them. However, I knew this time would be different. I felt it! I kept having this sickly feeling in the pit of my stomach with the reoccurring thought, *Cheryl, you need to leave.* Yet, I couldn't convince my dad to do so. My 'level of faith' wasn't anywhere near his, so I eventually stopped trying to persuade him, but I still kept packing.

CHAPTER 2

Exactly What I Need

Saturday, August 27, 2005

It was now Saturday morning. The school where I was teaching, Dunbar Elementary/Middle School, was scheduled to hold a parent orientation that morning. I reluctantly went, since the school was only six blocks away from where I lived. Only six teachers showed up, along with the principal. We all agreed that it would be wise to postpone the orientation until after the hurricane, so we posted signs on all of the gates around the school grounds stating, "Parent Orientation postponed due to hurricane." Then we left. Little did we know that the orientation was permanently postponed for the entire school year!

I had to run to the store to get a few more hurricane supplies like batteries, canned foods, ice and gas. It took much longer than I thought because the stores were running very low on these supplies and the lines were long everywhere I went. I had to go to several places to get what I needed, which became very frustrating. I finally ended up going to Walmart, the most recently built one on Tchoupitoulas Street. The store was extremely crowded as everyone was rushing around scrambling to get whatever they needed.

Much to my surprise, most of the shelves were almost empty. All I wanted was a pack of size "C" batteries. I searched EVERYWHERE in that store and found none! There were NO size "C" batteries anywhere in that store!

As one of the associates whizzed by me I caught her and asked, "Excuse me, Ma'am, but do you have any size "C" batteries in this store?"

She glanced at me and said, "If you don't see it on the shelves, we don't have it in the store," and she kept walking.

I wanted to scream! This was the fourth store I had been to and I still had no batteries! I was tired and I did not want to go to any more stores. I whispered a prayer, *Dear Father God, where are the batteries? Please help me find some size "C" batteries somewhere.*

I decided that since I could not find any batteries I'll just get whatever canned goods I could find. So I headed from one part of the store to another, maneuvering through the crowd, trying to get to the canned goods section. I chose the path of least resistance. I went toward the back of the store, passed the shoes, and went through the infant and toddler area. I assumed there would be fewer people in that part of the store. While passing by the baby strollers, I happened to glance down at one of the shelves and – lo' and behold— my eyes fell on a pack of size "C" batteries! A pack of eight size "C" batteries was tucked between two baby car seats! I mumbled to myself, *Lord God Almighty, this is amazing! It's exactly what I need in a place that I never would have expected to find it!* Does God answer prayer or what?

I snatched up the pack of batteries and held it close to my bosom as if were a newborn baby. Forgetting all about the canned goods, I turned and headed straight for the front of the store. I was darting through all the customers while cradling my precious cargo. Finally I made it to the front of the store and stood in what seemed to be an endless line. But I didn't mind the wait because I found my prized possession. As I stood in line I kept the batteries tucked tightly under my arm so no one would snatch them away from me. After standing in line for about twenty-five minutes, I made it safely out of the store and was finally on my way home. While in the car, I turned on the radio and listened to the news about how the city was implementing its voluntary evacuation plan. I had a good mind to leave then, but, like I said, my conscience wouldn't let me.

Sunday, August 28, 2005

We did not have church Sunday morning due to the impending hurricane. Most people were packing and heading out of the city anyway. The mayor finally called a mandatory evacuation for the city of New Orleans about 20 hours before the storm hit us. Those who did not have the means to get out of the city were evacuated to the Louisiana Superdome.

I received two very important phone calls that day. The first was from my Aunt Lona, my dad's sister. She's about 5'3" tall, with a dark chocolate complexion, shoulder length curly, black hair, and a very defined figure. She has five older brothers and she displays it in how she walks. She walks like a woman from the hood!

Aunt Lona was in the process of evacuating and was responsible for our 89-year-old Great Aunt Pee who, like my dad, did not want to leave the city either. Aunt Lona called Daddy so he could persuade Aunt Pee to evacuate.

At first Daddy got on the phone and asked Lona, "Leave the city? Why? Where is your faith?"

Then I quickly intervened on the phone and told him, "Daddy, forget the faith! Please tell Aunt Pee to get in the car with Lona. If they don't have faith to ride out this hurricane leave them alone!"

Much to my surprise, Daddy listened to me and told Aunt Pee to get into the car. She did and they left for Baker, Louisiana.

Meanwhile, I was still at home sick to my stomach when I got a call from my cousin Katrina, who lived not too far from one of the canals that was breached. She was in the process of evacuating also. A former theology student, she recently received her ministerial license. I told her about my plight of having to stay back with Daddy to ride out this storm. She said, "Cheryl, although you're staying behind, everything will be alright. It may not be easy, but it will be alright. God has it all in His hands and He will protect you." After a brief pause she added, "And another thing, turn off the radio and television and stop listening to the news!" When I did what she said, my anxiety was somewhat eased. By the way, after this hurricane we've considered calling my cousin by her middle name instead of her first name. The name "Katrina" actually means "to purify, cleanse."

CHAPTER 3

The Nightmare Begins

As Sunday night approached, the city began to feel the effects of Hurricane Katrina. The winds were so ferocious that it made the rain sound like bricks as it hit the house. All kinds of objects were blown through the neighborhood; lawn chairs, garbage cans, tree branches, aluminum storage shades, and street signs. Windows were blown out of high rise buildings. Store signs were ripped from their places of business and billboards were shredded into splinters. Trees were knocked into houses and almost every house had some type of roof damage from the winds. Amazingly, our house made it through the first nine hours of the storm with no damage that we were aware of. However, the electricity went out in our neighborhood at 5:57 Monday morning.

Monday, August 29, 2005

At 8 o'clock Monday morning my nightmare began. I woke up early and got dressed quickly. I didn't get much sleep the night before anyway. As I walked to the front of the house, I smelled a very heavy scent of rainwater. I thought, *why do I smell rainwater **inside** my house?* I came to the front and discovered that the wind had blown the front shutter wide open. The sofa and carpet were soaking wet on one side of the living room. I immediately slammed it shut. Then I heard something in the back of the house crash. I ran to the back to see what it was. One of the tiles had fallen from the ceiling in the kitchen.

The ceiling in our house is made of sheet rock. If the sheet rock stays in water too long it crumbles into sawdust. That is what was happening to the ceiling on one side of our house. During the night water began seeping through the roof which dripped down onto the ceiling and settled into the sheet rock. Thus, the sheet rock was beginning to crumble. For the next several hours I spent most of my time cleaning up sheet rock! I was pacing through the house setting out buckets, pots, pans, bowls, all types of containers that could catch water as it leaked through the roof and made the ceiling crumble and fall in. Daddy was up by 9 a. m. and he was patiently assessing the damage.

My brother called us from Georgia and I answered the phone. He said, "Cheryl, how are you all doing down there?"

I responded, "Emile, just PRAY!" Then I hung up the phone and went back to cleaning up sheet rock.

A few minutes a later my youngest sister, Miriam, called and this time Daddy answered the phone. She asked, "Daddy, are you alright?"

Daddy jubilantly responded, "Oh, everything is going GOOD! We're doing just fine!"

I almost flew into a rage! I thought to myself, *What in the world is he talking about? Can't he see the ceiling is falling in and we are about to lose the roof on this house? What's wrong with the man?!!* Nevertheless, I didn't verbally respond to him. I just kept cleaning up sheet rock around the house.

About one half hour later Yolanda called. She asked, "Daddy, is everything OK?"

Once again Daddy answered gladly, "Yes, everything is ALL RIGHT!"

Finally I could stand it no longer. As he was talking to her I pulled the phone from his hand and said, "Daddy, why do you keep telling everyone that everything is going fine?" I spoke to Yolanda on the phone and said, "The ceiling is falling in on one side of the house and the roof is leaking. We have buckets, pots, pans and bowls all over the house to catch the water. I'm the one doing all the work while Daddy is calmly sitting down saying, 'All is well.'" I really began pouring out my heart to her and she patiently listened.

This situation reminded me of Mary and Martha in Luke 10:38 – 42. Martha was doing all the work while Mary was quietly sitting at Jesus' feet; her full attention was on Him. I was frantically running around the house while my dad just sat and watched everything happen. It's funny now that I think about it, although it wasn't funny then.

Monday, August 29, 2005, was probably the LONGEST day in my entire life! Since the electricity went out, we kept the radio on to stay abreast of the hurricane. I sat on my bed and listened to horror stories from people who were calling the station because they were in dire need of help. There was an elderly woman who called. Apparently, she lived alone and had to face the storm by herself. She was petrified and even as she spoke, one could hear the thunder, the tumultuous wind, and the heavy rain in the background pouncing upon her house.

She was frantically pleading with the D.J., "Please help me! Send someone to help me! I'm here all by myself and the water is coming in through the roof...!"

The D.J. interrupted her. "Ma'am, Ma'am, the rescue workers won't be able to get to you right now. The winds and the floodwaters are still too high and there's too much debris on the streets..." As he spoke, we heard a sudden crash – then static — **then a deafening silence. The silence was louder than the thunder from the hurricane!**

After a few seconds, the D.J. finally muttered, "Ma'am? Ma'am? Are – are you still there?" **There was no answer, only deafening silence.**

I quickly mustered up enough strength to dash across the room and click-off the radio. I could take no more! As I crawled back onto the bed I thought to myself, *why was she left to face the hurricane alone? Who's responsible for her? Isn't she someone's grandmother, or mother, or sister, or aunt? Didn't anyone think to check on her before the hurricane began? Or maybe someone did try to persuade her to leave, but she chose to stay because she felt that she could ride out the storm – just like most of the elderly did.*

Time moved on and as each minute passed it seemed like eternity. I continued my duty of setting out containers to catch the water falling from the ceiling. After a while I turned on the radio once again to make the time pass faster. We finally heard the reporter say, "The worst of the storm should be over by about 12 noon for the city of New Orleans. The heavy winds and rain should begin dying down by then." I breathed a sigh of relief and whispered a prayer. "Thank You Lord, we're finally getting to the end of this thing." By about 1 p.m. most of the winds began to subside and the heavy rain turned into drizzle just like the reporter said. The weather remained that way from the evening into the night. However, by this time, the floors on one side of our house were soaking wet and the sky could be seen through certain sections of our roof.

Eventually, most of the cell phones across the city started going out. A user could receive calls coming in but could not make any going out. Since there was no electricity, nighttime came quickly so we went to bed early, at about 7:30 or 8 p.m. I slept in the front bedroom under an open window with a cool breeze blowing across my face. The stars were very beautiful that night. I noticed that our neighborhood was unusually quiet so I thought we were the only household that did not evacuate.

Before going to bed, Daddy and I examined the water level around our house. It was up to the headlights on his car and up to the door handles on my car. There was a minimal amount of flood water going into our neighbor's house across the street, maybe two inches or so. Their house was the lowest in our area. All the other houses in our block were high, dry and safe. All was well. The neighborhood was peaceful that night. However, as I was on my way to sleep I kept thinking about that poor elderly woman who was left alone to face the storm by herself.

Tuesday, August 30, 2005

I woke up early Tuesday morning, got dressed, and as I glanced out the window, I noticed that the water level seemed to be higher than it was the night before. I went to the back of the house and looked out the door to examine our vehicles. The water was now on the hood of both cars! It was climbing onto the steps and porches of the houses in our block. When I saw this, my heart almost skipped a beat. I thought, *my God, this water is rising! But it can't be rising because the hurricane is OVER! The flood waters are supposed to GO DOWN after a hurricane, NOT RISE! If there was a 25 foot tidal surge it would have arrived with the tail of the hurricane, not 12 – 18 hours later.*

I picked up the phone to call my family in Georgia and the phone was DEAD! **There was NOTHING–except that deafening silence again–a silence that was louder than thunder!** My heart dropped down to my toes! You see, being able to stay in touch with my family members during the storm gave me hope because I still had communication with the outside world. However, once the phone was dead I felt isolated. I did not want to be cut off from the rest of the world and die in rising flood waters. No one knew where we were, nor could they get to us! I ran to the back of the house, woke Daddy up, and told him to pack his bags because the water was rising. We had to leave! He looked outside, saw how the water had risen, and started packing.

Meanwhile, I turned on the radio to try to find an explanation for this phenomenon of rising water. I discovered that *all but one* of the radio stations had lost power overnight. Only WWL was still up and running. The D.J. at this station, Garrett Robinson, was receiving text messages from people who were telling horror stories about how they woke up to find water rushing into their homes. In some areas of the city, the water was rising so fast that many people didn't have time to evacuate, be rescued, or pack their bags. Many died, trapped inside their homes and attics. Many drowned.

Ninth Ward residents were especially vulnerable to the rushing flood water. The Dawson family experienced this devastation first hand. Debra was a thirty-three year old single mom with four children ranging from the ages of five to fifteen. She did not have the means to leave the city before the hurricane and she did not want to take her four children to the Superdome either. Therefore, she stayed at home to ride out the storm. Her forty-year old brother, Lance, decided to stay with them for protection.

Debra said that her family went to bed that night with no problems. However, during the night they began hearing crackling and gurgling sounds. At first they didn't know what it was because the house was very dark so they could not see anything. When her brother, Lance, got up to investigate, he put his feet on the floor and was shocked when he stepped into five inches of water! He immediately alerted everyone else in the house. They didn't have time to grab any extra clothes. They only had enough time to quickly move to higher ground because the water was rushing in at the rate of about two inches per minute. Lance tore a hole in the ceiling and began putting family members into the attic. They all were finally safe in the attic, but as they were scurrying in the dark trying to get to the roof, the two youngest children, ages five and eight, fell from the attic back into the water below. The two panic-stricken children almost drowned so Uncle Lance raced back into the water to rescue them. He carried them up to the attic once again, but it put a strain on his heart and he died of a heart attack shortly thereafter. The family had to leave his body there in the attic as they sat on the rooftop in the dark, drizzling rain waiting for the helicopter rescue workers.

Rising waters *after* the hurricane! This caused many people to panic! It caused pandemonium and chaos to break out in our city! The flood waters were rising throughout the city and initially no one had an explanation as to *why* it was happening. Eventually we learned that the 17th Street Levy was breached, along with several other levees in the New Orleans area, and this is what caused the flooding.

While listening to the radio, I went throughout the house gathering all of our most valuable possessions and placed them on the highest shelves and elevated places in our house. Daddy finally came from the back of the house with the one bag he packed. We both sat on the front porch and waited for our rescue as we watched the water rise.

CHAPTER 4

Meet Our Friendly Neighbors

We sat from about 9:30 that morning until about 4 that evening waiting for our rescue. Helicopters were flying throughout the entire city. About every 20 minutes or so two or three would fly over our neighborhood. I tried to flag them down each time but I never got their attention. I later learned that those helicopters were transporting patients from Tulane University Hospital to other medical facilities in Louisiana.

I was wrong about Daddy and I being the only household in our neighborhood that did not evacuate. I soon discovered that most of the people in our area stayed home and tried to ride out the storm. As we waited, I began to see more and more families leave their homes and wade through the flood water trying to find higher ground. They were floating on whatever they could find, car tires, doors, large plastic tubs, slabs of styrofoam, even holding onto tree branches. They were all headed for the Shell Gas Station on Carrollton Avenue, which was about eight blocks away. As they passed our house, they greeted us and we'd give directions to them about how to walk through the water without being over-whelmed so that they could get safely to Carrollton Avenue. Some of them asked us if we needed any help and I'd mention to them that because of Daddy's wheelchair we needed a boat to get out of the neighborhood. The water level was already up to the average person's chest and shoulders as they tried to walk through it. Soon we began to see several boats coming through the neighborhood, some with paddles and some motorized.

After a while, our very friendly next-door neighbor, Darrell, came outside. I was very surprised to see that he was even still at home! He was about my age with brown-skin, thin build, and approximately 5'6" tall. His face was trimmed with a thin mustache and a goatee. Whenever he spoke, one had to listen very carefully because he spoke very fast, but he also had a severe stammering problem. He looked like he couldn't hurt a fly! He was single, free, disengaged, and did not have the responsibility of caring for anyone else but himself. So I wondered why he had not fled the area before the storm came. Darrell had a lucrative, successful, private pharmaceutical business in the back of his house with a faithful clientele of all ethnic backgrounds from across the city of New Orleans. He provided quality service 24/7. He had connections! If he wanted to evacuate, he certainly could have! His business partner's name was Rawly, who was also his foot runner. Rawly was about 5'10", dark skin, stocky, with a low-cropped hair cut. Together the two of them were an amazing team.

Darrell absolutely adored my daddy and would do anything for him – except give up his pharmaceutical business! During the twenty or so years that he lived next door to us, he gave Daddy Christmas gifts, had our grass cut, had our house sprayed for rodents, and from time to time kept Daddy company as they sat on the front porch. He was always doing nice things for Daddy.

The hours ticked on as we watched the water rise inch by inch and watched all the other neighbors leave the neighborhood. Morning turned into afternoon and afternoon turned into evening and still no motorized rescue boat came for us. I kept trying to figure out why Darrell was still hanging around the neighborhood. Was he still there just to guard his pharmaceutical products? Then it dawned on me! Could it be that Darrell wanted to be sure that my daddy got out of the neighborhood safely first before he left? *(God save his soul!)* So I mentioned to Darrell that Daddy wanted a 'motorized' boat to take him out of the neighborhood. Thus, Darrell called his business partner, Rawly, and whispered something into his ear. Rawly left the house for a while.

Within an hour, a neighbor by the name of Lowell came directly to our house with a motorized boat to pick us up. (I told you Darrell had connections!) Lowell was a burly, brown skin guy, about six feet tall, with a crew cut. He looked sort of like a panda bear. He and several other men from our neighborhood formed makeshift search and rescue teams for the distressed families in our area who could not get out on their own. These groups of men found boats lying idle in our neighborhood and "borrowed" them to help others who were trapped in their homes. They were collecting families and taking them to dry ground. Finally, it was our turn to be rescued! The men put Daddy and me into the boat, along with our two duffle bags, and drove farther into the neighborhood to get other distressed families before going to higher ground. We picked up an elderly woman and her dog that was crippled with arthritis. We also picked up a younger woman who was attached to a breathing apparatus along with her ten year old daughter. Then we headed to the Shell Gas Station on Carrollton Avenue.

At this point I must pause to mention something. **There are probably hundreds of unsung heroes that have risen to the occasion during this storm. They don't have Public Relations Managers to get them on TV to publicize the great things they've done to help hurricane victims. They don't have the clout to televise how they risked their lives** to save hundreds of others yet they themselves were still victims of the hurricane. But they are still heroes and my hat goes off to them!

CHAPTER 5

Shell Island

We arrived at the Shell Gas Station at about 5 p.m. As we approached it, I saw many of the neighbors who passed our house earlier already camped there. This gas station became our neighborhood island. It provided an estimated 500 square feet of dry ground. Many who were brought there had some type of physical limitation. Some were partially paralyzed, some had severe breathing problems, some had walkers, some wheelchairs, and there were even two v e r y p r e g n a n t women! It was a very social place. It actually reminded me of a nightclub. People who may not have gotten along or even noticed each other under a different set of circumstances were now socializing due to a common crisis. Dozens of families who were rescued within our neighborhood came to the Shell Gas Station initially but they didn't stay very long. As evening fell, they migrated four blocks down the street to Lafayette Elementary School because they did not want to spend the night on a concrete slab exposed to all the elements. They sought an indoor shelter instead.

There was an ambulance stranded at the station. The driver was having some mechanical problems and did not want to take a chance driving through the high flood water, so he parked for the evening and waited for the water to recede. The ambulance provided light for the entire area, which was good since there were no streetlights. Helicopters were constantly flying overhead throughout the night so the emergency medical workers sent out several SOS signals to them. I assume they made contact at some point although we saw no evidence of it.

As darkness fell over our concrete island, the loud friendly chatter minimized to soft whispers. Daddy sat in his wheelchair and went to sleep. I laid down on the ground and used my duffle bag as a pillow. Once again the weather was cool and breezy and the stars were absolutely beautiful. As I was dozing off to sleep it suddenly dawned on me, *Cheryl, you're homeless! You're sleeping outside on concrete with a bunch of strangers, exposed to the elements! Now you know what it's like to be homeless.* Then I remembered the hundreds of nights in times past when I was in my own comfortable, warm bed, at my own house with my own pillow and blanket, and just before I'd doze off to sleep I'd whisper, "Thank You Lord for a warm, safe place to sleep that I can call my own." Then I'd fall asleep. As I lay on the concrete that night, I may have been temporarily homeless, but I wasn't hopeless.

CHAPTER 6

You Can't Take It with You

Wednesday, August 31, 2005

The morning started off slow and quiet as the Shell Island Campers woke up. The emergency medical workers packed up the ambulance and went on their way. The weather began to return to its typical New Orleans routine, hot and humid. When we woke up we noticed that our island had shrunk overnight. Apparently, the water was still rising in other areas of the city and now it was coming up into the Shell Gas Station. Our 500 square feet of concrete was getting smaller.

There was a lot of looting going on that day. Even before Daddy and I arrived at the Shell Station looters had already gotten into the building and ravaged everything. Whatever the hurricane left standing, looters demolished it! They tore up Walgreens! They broke into all the stores on Carrollton Avenue and in the Carrollton Shopping Center. They proudly walked down the streets, through flood water, rolling baskets loaded with stolen goods: televisions, CD's and VCR's, camcorders, microwave ovens, racks and racks of clothing, jewelry, shoes – all types of things they didn't need and would never be able to use!

I thought to myself, *where are they taking it to? Where will they hide all this stuff? When will they ever get a chance to use it? If they were rescued from the storm, surely they couldn't pack all this stuff up and take it with them.* **You can't take it with you.** I was utterly amazed to see the greed of man in full bloom! It was beyond reason! What in the world could they do with all that? AMAZING! They even ravaged Popeye's and Wendy's, two fast food places! I thought to myself, *if the chicken isn't already fried and the burgers aren't already done. why are they taking the food in the first place? Will they take it home and cook it themselves? There's no gas or electricity at home! Everyone's house is flooded. Where will they store all that stuff in a flood?*

Not everyone was driven by greed, however. Many were sharing their goods with those who had absolutely nothing, those who had to leave their homes quickly and did not have time to pack anything. As a matter of fact, that afternoon we had a downright picnic on Shell Island. There were sandwiches, salads, snacks and games like chess, checkers, and cards. For a while, many people were having so much fun they almost forgot they needed to be rescued!

As the day progressed, several campers realized they would not be able to sleep on the island for a second night. The water was coming in too fast and the island kept getting smaller. More and more campers migrated to the elementary school four blocks down the street. But where would daddy and I go and how would we get there? I couldn't roll daddy through the flood water, which was now waist deep and becoming very murky.

Not only did I want to get off the island, but I wanted to leave New Orleans—immediately! I did not just want to go to another shelter. I wanted to go to a location where they were transporting people **out** of the city – like the airport! I tried to explain this matter to Daddy, but he had a different mindset. He wanted to remain in the vicinity of our house because that was his comfort zone. He wanted the water to recede so he could go back home. I thought, *go back home! What home? We have no home to go back to!* We had an extremely intense discussion about it and could not come to an agreement.

Shortly thereafter Mr. Bob, one of our neighbors who lived two doors down from us, came to talk to Daddy and me. Mr. Bob was about 6'4" tall with pepper gray hair and an oblong face. He was a tall, slinky, caramel toned man, in his early sixties. He had a deep, thundering baritone voice, which made it nearly impossible for him to whisper. Whenever he spoke, everyone in the neighborhood knew he was talking. He said he had some relatives who owned a social hall in a two story building. They were taking in elderly people and those with physical limitations who had no place else to go. We were invited to spend the night. This was an answer to Daddy's prayer and he gladly accepted the invitation but I had my reservations. Mr. Bob sent a boat for us and once again we were transported to a different location.

43

CHAPTER 7

Our Second Story Shelter

We were taken to a two story building, a make shift evacuation center that was formally a wedding hall. There were 17 steps going from the first floor to the second floor. The first eight stairs were already under water so several men had to carry Daddy up the steps. On the second floor was a large room, approximately sixty feet long by forty-five feet wide. There were a few cots along the walls and some lounge chairs in the room. The back of the building contained a kitchen, three offices, two restrooms and several large storage rooms. The kitchen was well stocked with plenty of food. The counters were covered with canned goods stacked high along the walls. All types of beverages, including water, were stored in several coolers on the floor and there were tables full of snacks. (Of course our neighborhood supermarket involuntarily donated all these groceries to our cause.)

The people who owned the business were a sister-brother team, Ms. Ellen and Mr. Oscar. They were very gracious hosts and tried to make us feel as comfortable as possible. Ms. Ellen was a very jubilant woman, probably in her early fifties, approximately 5'5" tall, thin build, with an olive complexion, and a smile that could light up an entire room.

Mr. Oscar, also in his fifties, was about six feet tall, thin build, with dark brown wavy hair and a small mustache, a dark chocolate complexion and eyes that made him look like he was always smiling. There were eighteen other people in that building with Daddy and me—thirteen males and seven females altogether. Several of them were elderly or had physical limitations.

The first night we were there it was extremely hot and everyone was miserable. As a matter of fact, it was warmer inside the building than it was outside. I asked Ms. Ellen if I could wash up a little. She said, "Sure," and gave me a twenty ounce bottle of water and a piece of cloth. I did miraculous things with that water and washcloth. At first I didn't think it was possible to "take a bath" with such a small amount of water, but I managed. I even had enough water left over to brush my teeth!

Twenty of us had to share two restrooms with no running water! In order to flush the toilet we had to carry a five gallon or ten gallon bucket down the stairs, fill it with flood water, haul it back upstairs, and pour it into the toilet. (This really helped me learn to appreciate the modern conveniences of life, like indoor plumbing and a toilet that flushes!) After two days, however, the flood water in the front of the building became so filthy and murky that it stopped up one of the toilets. So we were able to use only one toilet instead and in order to flush it we hauled water from the back of the building, where it was somewhat cleaner.

Thursday, September 1, 2005

There was a generator on the premises but there was no gas to put in it. Therefore, Thursday morning our neighborhood pharmacist and his business partner, Darrell and Rawly, took it upon themselves to go through the neighborhood to find some gas. After about two hours the dual came back with a few gallons of gas. The generator was hooked up, filled with gas and *–voila–* we had electricity! Once we had electricity, we turned on the fifty-inch fan and finally had air! We plugged in the six-inch black and white television and watched the news. Those with cell phones began recharging them. We were rollin'! One gallon of gas provided enough electricity for about two hours and ten minutes then it would be refilled so we could have more electricity.

For the next three days our daily routine consisted of listening to the news, eating, reading, playing cards, trying to contact relatives, watching television and trying to figure out a way to escape from New Orleans. I spent much of my time writing in my diary. This was my therapy, my way of coping with the situation.

At some point during the week it felt as if an atmosphere of despair engulfed the entire city. We all felt like mice trying to escape from a mousetrap! We heard reports about the riots in the Superdome and how multiplied thousands of people were packed into that building which eventually had no electricity. Our two-story makeshift shelter was a luxury compared to what they were going through! We listened as the mayor of New Orleans and the president of Jefferson Parish lashed out against the federal government and the president of the United States for not responding swiftly enough to the disaster.

The sound of helicopters swarming around the city became routine, almost hypnotic. They would swoop down, rescue a group of people then take them off somewhere. Since we were in a two-story building, we could see much of what was going on in the neighborhood. We witnessed a helicopter rescue one block from where we were. Early Thursday afternoon a young mother and her two young children were air lifted from their apartment. However, later that evening we saw that same young woman and her two children back at that same apartment. We wanted to know what happened.

We soon discovered that those who were being rescued were taken to the Causeway Bridge and dropped off there. They were waiting for buses to transport them from the bridge to the airport. However, it was hot on the bridge and there was nothing to protect them from the sun. Many people had been waiting there for more than three days and some were already sickly and could not withstand the heat. The woman said there were numerous corpses sprawled across the bridge and she did not want her children exposed to that environment so she came back home.

That was the typical scene around the city. People were being rescued from the flood waters that engulfed their homes and then dropped off on bridges, overpasses and highways only to be stranded there for several days at a time without water, food, shelter, or medication. Under these conditions, numerous citizens died.

On Thursday evening the cell phones began working again, even if only for a few minutes. I asked Mr. Oscar if I could use his cell phone to call our relatives in Georgia. They had not heard from us in three days and I knew they were worried about us. He let me use his cell phone so I called my sister and had a 30 second conversation with her. I spoke as quickly as possible and told her where we were and how we were making plans to try to get out of New Orleans by Saturday morning. She was surprised and glad to hear my voice. Daddy and I later learned that my brother, who is in the military, was making plans to come down to New Orleans in a military truck and execute a search and rescue effort for us if they had not heard from us within the next 24 hours. I'm glad I called and made contact with them before he got to that point.

CHAPTER 8

Dealing with Despair

Friday, September 2, 2005

By Friday morning everyone was getting very antsy. We were desperate to get out of the city of New Orleans. A few people in the shelter finally contacted some relatives and made plans for their relatives to meet them at some specified location to take them out of the city. Their plans were successful and they were gone by Friday night. However, the rest of us were trying to figure out a way to get out of the city without having to go to the Superdome or stand on the Causeway Bridge or some other highway in the scorching sun waiting for a bus to pick us up. There were guard stations set up throughout the metro area and no one could come in or go out as they pleased without showing some form of identification.

On Friday afternoon at about 11 a.m. we noticed that a fire had broken out on Carrollton Avenue about three blocks from our building. It started across the street from the Notre-Dame Seminary. The red and orange flames rose fiercely and heavy black smoke billowed from the area. At first two or three helicopters tried to put it out by flying over it while dropping a few buckets of water but that was utterly useless.

They quickly gave up and went back to their rescue efforts. We watched the fire throughout the day as the flames jumped from one building to the next, consuming everything in its path. I began praying, "Lord please don't let that fire come this way. Don't let there be an explosion. Please let it stay contained within that block!" There was a restaurant and a portrait shop within that block and all the fire needed was some oil or gas to give it more energy and cause an explosion. The flames went down Carrollton Avenue and burned up everything, then turned the corner and started burning the buildings on Pritchard Street for a while, and when it was finished with that block, it turned the corner again and burned everything on Dublin Street. It finally got to Fig Street and burned itself out. The flames raged for about eighteen hours, from 11 a.m. Friday afternoon until about 5a.m. Saturday morning, when the last amber burned itself out. By Saturday morning, the entire square block was nothing but rubble and ashes.

I tried to talk to daddy again about us leaving the city and heading for Georgia, but he was not willing to go that far. He preferred to go to Grandpa's house. My 93-year-old grandfather lived just off of Tchoupitoulas Street, two blocks away from the Mississippi River. We heard on the news that it was one of the few places in the city that did not get any flood water. However, we could not contact Grandpa on the phone. The farthest place Daddy was willing to go was to Baker, Louisiana, where his relatives lived close by, and he could get back into the city quickly and easily if necessary. No matter how much Daddy and I discussed this matter, we could not come to an agreement on this issue. Daddy kept saying, "We should be praying for God's will to be done — nevertheless, not my will, but Thy will be done."

This really screwed up my thinking! Of course I wanted God's will to be done, as long as His will was that we'd leave New Orleans and never return! Of course I wanted His will to be done, as long as it included getting out of the city as soon as possible! I was thinking, *surely it isn't God's will for us to stay in New Orleans and die in this flood. I have too much to live for! I have too much life left in me! I can't die here! Surely it could not have been God's will for us to stay in a city where there's no electricity and no clean running water, where the water is so filthy that it's toxic!*

I did a lot of soul searching and self examination that Friday night as I was trying to go to sleep. As a matter of fact, I couldn't go to sleep at all. I kept thinking about the movie, The Diary of A Young Girl. Have you ever seen the movie or read the book? It is the story of a young Jewish girl who lived in the nineteen thirties and forties, during the time when Hitler was gathering all the Jews and putting them in concentration camps. Anne Frank and her family, along with a few other people, were hidden in an upper room to escape Hitler's fury. They were eventually discovered, however, and taken to a concentration camp. But while Anne was hidden she kept a diary. Anne's father survived the concentration camp, came back to the upper room where his family was hidden, and found her diary. The movie and the book are actually based on her notes.

Anyway, as I was praying that night, I told the Lord, "I don't want to be like Anne Frank. I don't want to die here and let someone else find my diary and later tell my story. Lord, please let me live to tell my own story." I kept repeating to myself, **"I shall not die but live, and declare the works of the Lord!" (Psalm 119:17)** I prayed, "Dear Heavenly Father please get us out of this hell hole!" All I wanted to do was get out of the building and go straight to the airport, without any hindrances, detours, or delays! Even after praying I still could not go to sleep, so I began to sing every praise song I could think of – any song that came to mind.

O Come Let Us Adore Him
The Steadfast Love of the Lord Never Ceases
Great Is Thy Faithfulness
I Need Thee Every Hour
Holy, Holy, Holy
All Hail the Power of Jesus' Name
Awesome God
To Him Who Sits On the Throne
Jesus, Name Above All Names
Yes, Jesus Loves Me
Oh, How I Love Jesus
O' How He Loves You and Me
Jesus, There's Something About that Name
God Has Smiled On Me

Why was I singing? Because I felt like I was not being heard! I felt ignored, overlooked, insignificant! I sang to put my mind and emotions at ease, to silence them, because I was confused, scared – f e a r f u l – and I had to encourage myself. I had to m a g n i f y the Lord and make Him bigger than all my anxieties. I had to remind myself of how GREAT God is compared to all my problems. Besides all this, I learned a very important secret over the years. *If you want Almighty God to show up in your situation nothing gets His attention like worship!* So I went on and on singing one song after another until I finally sang myself to sleep.

CHAPTER 9

The Resolve

Saturday, September 3, 2005

Saturday morning everyone in the shelter woke up and began cleaning and packing. Some people knew where they were headed because they made plans. But Daddy and I had no idea of where we were going or how we'd get there because we had not come to any agreement. There were now only fourteen people left to evacuate the shelter.

Mr. Oscar contacted one of his cousins, Malcolm, a licensed boatman, to transport us from the shelter to any place where we could be bussed out of the city or taken to the airport. Malcolm was a heavy-set, charcoal-toned man, who looked to be in his mid forties. He was about 6'3" tall, with a round face and weighed about 350 pounds. Whenever he walked the entire room shook.

It amazes me that even in the midst of no electricity or running water Mr. Oscar and his family had the calm, focus of mind and resources to stay in contact with each other and help their neighbors! You could tell they were experts in the hospitality industry. They made sure others were comfortable in spite of the circumstances.

That afternoon, at about 11a.m., Malcolm came with his crewmen and two motorized boats. Nine of the fourteen people were loaded onto the boats. They would have to return later to get the others. Five passengers were loaded onto the first boat while Daddy and I, along with two other people, got on the second one. Of course Daddy was carried while I had to wade through chest deep water to get on board. I did notice, however, that the water had receded over the past four days. Now it was only up to the fifth step instead of the eighth step.

The boats headed back through the neighborhood instead of traveling down Carrollton Avenue or taking another expressway, since this was a quicker route out of the city. As we were being transported, I had an eerie feeling of being in a third world country. It was five days after the hurricane but the water was still very high, about eight feet or so. The boat drivers had to be careful not to run into any parked cars. As a matter-of-fact, we couldn't even see where most of the cars were parked because they were completely submerged. Many houses were unrecognizable due to the extensive damage and I could see the despair in our neighbors' faces as they stood on their porches and watched us pass them on the boat. It felt like the end of the world!

We slowly approached the block where our house was and the scene became surreal. Although our house already stood five feet above the ground, the water had risen to the middle of our front door and my car was completely underwater. There was filth and debris everywhere. We saw large, broken tree branches, garbage cans, shingles from rooftops, wood and aluminum siding from homes, lawn furniture, old one gallon plastic containers and garbage bags floating in the water. It seemed like all the trash in our neighborhood floated to our corner.

I took one last hard look at what used to be our home. Then the thought occurred to me. *Cheryl, you woke up this*

*morning and now everything is completely different. Nothing
is the same. The places you used to go to no longer exist. The
people you normally see everyday, you may never see again.
Your life has changed overnight. How will you handle this?*
It was an eerie feeling, yet I resolved that issue at that very
moment. I knew I'd never again reside in New Orleans. I've
lived there all my life and now it was no longer my home.
This was my opportunity for a new beginning.

The three influences that held me in the city – my dad,
my church, and my job—no longer had a grip on me. My
dad? He no longer had a house or rental property. All of his
children lived out-of-state, so he had no reason to stay in the
city. My church? I was the pianist and the keyboard player
at our church for nineteen years and nine months before
the storm. The church was located in the lower ninth ward,
which was the hardest hit area in the city. Everything in that
area was destroyed, and I realized that it would probably
be a very long time before anything is rebuilt or completely
restored there. My job? I was a kindergarten teacher in the
public school system. Even before the hurricane hit, the
school system was in shambles. There's no telling how long
it would be before the schools were able to function at full
capacity again. Finally, I was **free** from New Orleans! I had
a new lease on life!

The two motorized boats turned the corner and as far
as the eye could see there was water *everywhere!* Oleander
Street had become Oleander River. General Ogden Street
was now General Ogden Swamp. Hurricane Katrina caused
the Gulf Coast Waters and Lake Ponchartrain to join hands
and swallow our fishbowl. New Orleans had returned to
its original state – swampland—the state it was in before
brothers Iberville and Bienville began settling here.

CHAPTER 10

The Taste of Freedom

Malcolm, the boatman, took us up to the Palmetto Street Canal then turned onto Airline Highway. This was a very gruesome area. We ran upon a dead body, lying face down, floating in the water. From what I could tell, it was a middle-aged male, wearing blue jean overalls and a plaid shirt. The body was extremely bloated. We also saw dead dogs and dead birds floating around. We had to be careful of the power lines. The water was about twenty feet high in that area and we could not see the houses at all. All we could see were their rooftops.

The boats continued down Airline Highway. We were hesitant as we approached the Orleans/Jefferson Parish boundary because there were guards on duty – two young men dressed in uniforms. Both were clean-shaven, in their mid-twenties, muscular and about six feet tall. One had straight brown hair with light brown eyes. The other had coal black hair with a cream complexion. They stopped us to ask where we were going. Earlier that day we heard on the news that the sheriff of Jefferson Parish was checking ID's and he would not let anyone enter his parish unless they resided there. The New Orleans International Airport is located in Jefferson Parish, so if the guards did not let us pass, we could not get out of the city. I quietly prayed that the guards would not make us turn around and prevent us from crossing through Jefferson Parish because it was our only route to the airport. The guards were gracious to us. They let us continue on our route. Thank God!

Farther down the road more Jefferson Parish volunteers met us at the parish boundary. There were five older gentlemen who weren't wearing uniforms but had on orange reflective vests and were wearing ID badges. The afternoon sun beamed down on their bronze skin and blue eyes as they approached our boats. After asking us several questions, they helped us out of our boats, put us on the back of a pickup truck and drove us across the Causeway. WE WERE VERY SURPRISED TO SEE THAT THERE WAS NO WATER IN JEFFERSON PARISH! Airline Highway was completely dry in Metairie! The truck drove several miles down the highway and finally pulled over in front of a hotel/gas station, just a few miles away from the airport.

Everyone jumped out of the truck, pulled out their cell phones and started calling their relatives to come pick them up and take them to their destinations – everyone except Daddy and me. The truck driver noticed this so he asked us, "Where do you two want to go?" Daddy said he wanted to go to Baker, LA. But he needed a cell phone to call his sister — my Aunt Lona – to contact her about transportation, room and board. The truck driver offered us his phone and Daddy made the call, but Aunt Lona did not answer the phone! Daddy hung up, sorely disappointed. He said despondently, "Nobody's answering. I don't know anywhere else we can go except…"

I quickly spoke up. "Georgia! Daddy, we can go to Georgia! At least they're expecting us there." Daddy had a perplexed look on his face, but said nothing.

The truck driver responded, "Georgia? Then you need to go to the airport."

My heart jumped for joy when he said the magic word, *"airport!"* He drove us a few blocks farther down the road to a bus stop where a shuttle bus could pick us up. We waited for only a few minutes and the shuttle soon came. We got on and it took us all the way to the airport. Finally, we arrived at the place I longed to be – the airport! Hallelujah!

It was about 1p.m. when we reached the airport, which was in shambles! A place that is usually filled with important businessmen and excited tourists now looked like a war zone with tons of trash everywhere and multiplied thousands of people trying to exit the city all at the same time. There was a make-shift morgue on one side of the airport and a temporary emergency medical ward on the other side. The stench was unbearable! It smelled like death! It was the smell of vomit, old dried blood, formaldehyde, and thousands of people who had not bathed or washed in several days, all rolled together.

There were extremely long lines of people that twisted and wrapped around the entire facility. Since Daddy was disabled, we did not have to wait in those long lines. There was a separate line for handicap people so we by-passed all the delays. We were in line for about one hour and forty minutes. It moved rather quickly compared to the other lines.

Getting through security, on the other hand, was a painstaking ordeal since Daddy was in a wheelchair and I had to carry his walker. We had to unzip, unstrap, unbuckle, pull off, take down and set aside various articles of clothing just to get through the gate. Once we passed through security, we were allowed to "redress" and move on. We whizzed through the airport terminal and soon came upon more crowds and long lines, so once again we stood and waited. The National Guard sectioned off the crowd, divided us into smaller groups, and assigned us to specific gates to board designated airplanes. We occupied ourselves by watching the airplanes take off and land while waiting for our turn to leave the city.

The group that Daddy and I were in—about 150 people—was led downstairs, outside, to a Jet Blue aircraft. Those with special needs were allowed to board first. Volunteer workers approached Daddy and asked him if he needed assistance boarding the plane or could he board it by himself. Of course he needed assistance. As Daddy was boarding, he was taken out of his own wheelchair and given a wheelchair from the airport. I turned to one volunteer and specifically requested that Daddy's wheelchair be put on the luggage rack so that it would be on the same plane with us and he'll have his own wheelchair when we reached our destination. Somehow, that did not happen. Daddy's wheelchair never made it on the plane at all! It was left in New Orleans and this really upset both of us!

We started boarding the plane at about 5 p.m. It took almost forty minutes just for everyone to get on and get settled since there were so many disabled people in our group.

Finally the doors closed and the plane started down the runway. The roar of the engines became louder as the plane gained speed and ascended into the air. While ascending, I looked out the window at the city of New Orleans below me. I thought to myself, *I've just made it through a major catastrophe and my life was spared. I'm glad to have had this experience and live to tell about it. It will be a wonderful testimony to pass on to my children and grandchildren— that's if I ever decide to get married and start a family of my own someday. BUT I NEVER – EVER WANT TO GO THROUGH ANOTHER TRAUMATIC EXPERIENCE LIKE THAT AGAIN FOR THE REST OF MY LIFE!!!!*

CHAPTER 11

A Prepared Place

O nce the plane was safely in the air, the pilot greeted us and made an announcement that went something like this. "Ladies and gentlemen welcome to Jet Blue Airline. Please sit back and relax as we cruise to beautiful Salt Lake City, Utah. This flight is just over four hours long. We hope you enjoy the ride." Suddenly many of the passengers began whispering, "Did he say we're going to Salt Lake City? You mean we're not going to Houston or San Antonio? All the other evacuees that left New Orleans before us are headed to Texas. Are we bypassing Texas altogether? Why are we going to a different location?"

Some of the passengers had their hearts set on Texas and were sorely disappointed that they were not informed about the change before they boarded the plane. However, most of us didn't mind the unexpected change in destination because we were so glad to be leaving New Orleans! We were, after all, evacuees, and at this point we didn't have the opportunity to choose our own destination anyway. We just had to go wherever they were taking us.

Traveling on the Jet Blue Airliner was sheer luxury! It was first class all the way! The flight attendants treated us royally. We were served a full course meal, not just peanuts and a drink, since travel time would be more than four hours. Each passenger had his/her own television screen, headset and reclining seat. We could choose our own television program or lay back and watch a movie. I decided to watch the news. Of course, the national headlines were all about how Hurricane Katrina devastated Southeast Louisiana and parts of Mississippi. Now I was seeing the hurricane from the view of an observer, not as one who was involved. I saw what the rest of America was seeing. Although I had an overhead, satellite view of the destruction, I began to realize something. Television is a very dynamic and important medium for transporting information, yet it could not convey the extensive turmoil and anguish that the hurricane victims experienced. I can't even begin to imagine what those people trapped in Manhattan, New York experienced on 911.

There was an elderly gentleman sitting on the plane behind me and, apparently, he felt the same way about the news coverage. As he was watching the broadcast, he began sharing his experience. I heard him say, "My wife and I made it through the storm together. We survived the night, but she was already ill even before the storm. We went to bed in each other's arms, but when I woke up the next morning she was dead. She died in my arms. When the rescue workers came, they took me, but they had to leave her behind in the house. I really miss my wife," he said as his voice cracked. My heart went out to that man.

Our plane landed in Salt Lake City, Utah just before 10 p.m. Saturday night. We were loaded onto several shuttle buses and taken for a 40 minute ride to Camp Williams, a military facility just outside the city. Our group of 150 people was the first set of evacuees to arrive at this site and the citizens were very excited to have us. The military personnel and volunteers brought us into a gymnasium, welcomed us, and sat us down for orientation. They laid out the three golden rules. "(1) Smoking is not allowed inside any of the buildings. If anyone wants to smoke, he/she must step outside to do so.

(2) Alcohol is strictly prohibited on the premises. Anyone caught with liquor will be arrested, no questions asked! (3) Military curfew – No one on the base is allowed on the streets before 6 a.m. or after 10 p.m. Ladies and gentlemen, welcome to beautiful Salt Lake City, Utah. We hope you enjoy your stay here."

After that, they registered us. Each of us had our snapshot taken. We were assigned a number and given a photo ID badge to wear that contained our name, height, weight, hair color, eye color and date of birth. We were to wear these badges at all times while on the base. Each of us was given an evacuee personal care package; that's a box and a bag that contained personal necessities like toothpaste, toothbrush, soap, washcloth, comb, razor, mouthwash, deodorant, etc. The box contained assorted snacks, fruit and beverages. They also provided pajamas and a change of clothes. Everything was laid out for us. We were in a ***prepared place***!

We were assigned to a specific building and escorted to our barracks. The barracks that Daddy and I were in could house about 20 people, but only seven were assigned to sleep there the first night. I was assigned a room with Daddy and four other men who were also wheelchair bound. I went into the room and began unpacking my duffle bag. I was about to change my clothes when I looked around and saw the other men staring at me. Then it hit me. *I am the ONLY female in a room with five other men*! I DON'T THINK SO!!! I quickly gathered all of my things and moved to an empty room down the hall. So I had a room all to myself that first night.

I had the luxury of taking a full shower – using as many gallons of water as necessary, instead of being limited to a 20 ounce bottle. It had been six whole days since I had a bath of any kind and it was exhilarating to be completely clean!

It was a pleasure to finally be able to brush all of the fuzz off of my teeth that had accumulated on them over the past few days.

I would like to report that I slept well that night, but I did not. I slept for a short period of time, maybe 3 ½ hours, because I had nightmares about the flooding in New Orleans and I kept hearing the sound of helicopters flying overhead. I found myself jumping up out of a sound sleep, landing in bed on my hands and knees muttering, "Where's the water? How high is the water? Are the helicopters here yet? When will someone come to rescue us?" Little did I realize, it would be several days before I got a solid night's sleep again.

CHAPTER 12

Jubilee! Release!

Sunday, September 4, 2005

Sunday morning in Salt Lake City, Utah was like a new breath of hope for many hurricane evacuees! Many evacuees had never seen mountains in real life before. The weather was sunny, cool and breezy, and we were mesmerized by the scenery. Just looking at those mountains was a good form of therapy for many of us because it brought such tranquility. We had embarked upon a whole new world! We felt as if we had just come from hell and made it into heaven.

Psalm 19: 1-4 "The heavens declare the glory of God and the skies show forth His handiwork. Day and night they tell about God. There is no speech nor language where their voice is not heard. Yet, their message goes throughout the whole earth."

As for me, although I had been to Salt Lake City before, I was still reminiscing about the handiwork of God. Think about it. Just twenty-four hours ago I was so scared that I had to sing myself to sleep. Thirty hours ago I was watching a raging fire engulf an entire city block and praying that it be contained and keep its distance. *Yesterday I was trying to escape from a city that is seven feet below sea level AND twenty feet underwater – a swampland! Today I'm in a place that's 4,000 feet above sea level, and it's the second driest state in America!* **Does God have a sense of humor or what?**

I did a lot of walking as I explored my new surroundings during my first day at Camp Williams. I found a quiet spot near a gate a*t* the edge of the camp. It was a cliff overlooking the highway below. I had a private time of prayer there. The thought occurred to me, *this is Jubilee – a time of release—a time of freedom—a chance to begin anew—a fresh start! I am no longer bound by the past because the past is buried underwater – literally!* I remembered the conversation I had with my sister two weeks before the hurricane. We were discussing the Year of Jubilee – the 50th year – a year of new beginnings! I asked the Lord, "Can this really be? Can I really have a new lease on life? I left so much chaos, trash and confusion in New Orleans." Then a bible verse came to my mind.

(Isaiah 43: 18-19) "Remember not the former things, neither consider the things of old. Behold I do a new thing. It shall spring forth and shall you not know it?" Yes!!! Now I have a new lease on life! I was elated! I ran back to the barracks as excited as I could be!

During our time at Camp Williams, I waited on Daddy hand and foot because I was so full of excitement that I didn't know what else to do with myself. I was just bubbling over with energy! I spent my time washing, drying and folding loads of clothes, running errands, bringing meals to Daddy, helping him get dressed and keeping his area organized, etc. (I think I was making all the other men in his room rather envious.) Periodically, I would overhear them making comments like, "Man, he's really lucky!" Of course, Daddy would quickly correct them and say, "No, I'm *blessed*, not lucky."

Each of those men had a story to tell about their families, or about why they were in their wheelchairs. One of them, Mr. Lewis, was a Vietnam War veteran. Mr. James, who had severe muscle spasms from time to time, was an embittered divorcee who was also abandoned by his children. One man was involved in a shoot out at a bar and lost his leg. Besides being in wheelchairs, they all had something else in common. Somehow, they had all lost contact with their families over the years.

On Sunday afternoon, I realized that my family in Georgia had not heard from us in three days. They were probably worried by now. I began searching the military base for a public telephone. **I discovered that there was only one public phone on the entire base!** It was located outside the Communications Building and **there was a very long line of people waiting to use it!** I prayed, "Dear God, I need to contact my family and that line is sooo l- o- n- g! Lord, where can I get to a phone?" I kid you not! Within 30 seconds after I whispered that prayer a young lady by the name of Jene' walked up to me and introduced herself. She was very petite, probably in her mid-twenties, with shoulder-length, straight, sandy-brown hair that was parted down the middle, and gentle blue eyes.

Jene' asked, "Are you an evacuee from the Gulf Coast?"

I answered, "Yes, I am."

She continued, "Do you want to use my cell phone so you can call your family?"

I could not believe my ears! **Does God answer prayer or what?!** You might call this a 'coincidence,' but I call it a **Divine Appointment!**

I responded, "Y—ye—, yes! Thank you!"

Jene' continued, "I really feel for you guys. I know what you're going through. I was in Manhattan when 911 occurred." She explained that she lives in Salt Lake City and when she heard about hurricane victims coming to her city, she wanted to help out in any way she could.

As she continued to talk, I kept pondering the fact that she picked me out of an entire crowd of people and volunteered her phone to me! My mind also went back to how I just happened to **find** those size "C" batteries in Walmart. That was no coincidence either. Truly, God does answer prayer!

To make a long story short, the battery on her phone was so low that the call did not go through at that time. However, I gave her my sister's phone number and she promised me that she would contact my sister and tell her where Daddy and I were and that we were OK. She kept her promise.

On Sunday afternoon, the public telephone was finally free so I used the opportunity to make a call. I contacted my sister on the phone and although we did not have a long conversation, we had a meaningful one.

I said, "Hello, it's me, Cheryl. Daddy and I are in Salt Lake City, Utah."

She responded, "I know. A lady named Jene' called us earlier and told us where you were."

I continued. "Listen, I don't know how long we are going to be here or when we'll be able to leave. I'm trying to convince Daddy that he needs to stay in Georgia instead of trying to go back to New Orleans. He still wants…"

She interrupted me. "Cheryl, we had a family meeting last week and we've come to a conclusion. When Daddy comes to Georgia he's going to stay here whether he likes it or not—even if we have to tie him down, he's not leaving! You two shouldn't have been there for the hurricane in the first place! Don't worry. We'll straighten Daddy out when he gets here."

Those words were so soothing to me! Finally, somebody understood what I was going through! After the conversation, I ran back to the barracks and I couldn't wait to tell Daddy the "good" news.

As I was preparing Daddy for bed that evening, I casually mentioned to him, "Daddy, did I tell you that I finally made contact with your people in Georgia on the phone today?" Daddy said, "You did? What did you talk about?" I said, "I can't tell you. It's a surprise!" Daddy asked, "What do you mean you can't tell me? He paused for a moment then he asked, "Are they gonna beat me up when I get to Georgia?"

I responded, "Actually, you have a good butt whipping coming to you when you get to Georgia." All of the other men in the room laughed. I didn't even realize they were listening to our conversation.

Daddy continued, "You mean they're really gonna **make** me live there in Georgia with them?"

I said, "Yes, Daddy, they will. So you may as well get used to it. You'll be living in Georgia from now on. We're not moving back to New Orleans."

Then one of Daddy's roommates said, "Man, you ought to be glad! At least your kids want you around them. My kids kicked me to the curb. They don't even want me around."

Daddy shrugged his shoulders and said, "Well, I guess I give up. I'll just have to go live in Georgia."

I thought to myself, *finally, he surrendered!*

Monday, September 5, 2005

More and more busloads of evacuees were being transported from the Gulf Coast to Camp Williams, so all of the barracks began filling up very quickly. The new evacuees were welcomed, registered, given personal care packages, and informed about the three golden rules. Of course, there are always a few in the bunch who want to challenge the rules. One afternoon, several police cars rushed onto one of the barracks. A few minutes later, several young men were brought out of the building wearing handcuffs, escorted to the vehicles, and driven away. Although it was a relatively quiet scene, the event captured everyone's attention! We later learned that those young men were arrested for smuggling liquor onto the premises. Also, periodically, military personnel would randomly go through the barracks to check for evidence of smoking – looking for cigarette butts, ashes, etc. If any of these items were found, everyone in the barracks was questioned until the culprit was discovered. Then the necessary action was taken.

On Monday morning, the Communications Center became a **real** communications center. Several dozen telephones were installed inside the building to accommodate all the evacuees. Now, all we had to do was walk inside the building and wait no more than five minutes to use the telephone. The parking lot of the Communications Center had become a news media center. All the local news stations gathered there to televise evacuees who were willing to tell their stories. If anyone wanted to have their fifteen minutes of fame and glory, that was the time to do it.

I returned to our barracks on Monday afternoon, after running some errands. When I walked through the door, I noticed a woman sitting on the bed talking to Daddy. I wanted to know what was up.

Daddy introduced us. He said, "Cheryl, this is Nurse Amy."

I cordially greeted her. She was a middle-aged woman with a fragile appearance, speckled gray hair, and a very soft voice.

She said, "Hi Cheryl, I'm from the Salt Lake City Aging Services. I was talking to your father. I understand that he has diabetes and the meals served here on this base don't accommodate diabetics. We were considering moving him to a better facility that specifically caters to his needs."

I asked, "Where will you move him to?"

She said, "I'm not quite sure yet. There are a couple of nursing homes that I can contact. But wherever I take him, I'll give you a phone number and I'm sure the two of you can stay in touch."

I responded, "What do you mean, 'Stay in touch?' Are you saying that I can't go with him?"

She said, "Well, it is a nursing home. I'm not sure they'll have any place to put you."

Her statements brought a terrible thought to my mind. As Daddy and I traveled through this ordeal, we heard horror stories about how family members became separated from each other because one member had health issues and needed to be transported elsewhere to get adequate care. In the process, the lines of communication were completely cut off. Not only were family members unable to stay in contact with each other, but one had no idea of where the other was being taken to. I did not want that to happen with Daddy and me.

I thought about it for a moment then I said, "Ma'am, I'm sure you mean well. But the **only** reason I'm here now is because **he** wanted to stay in New Orleans and ride out the storm, so I stayed with him. Otherwise, I definitely would've evacuated ahead of time. The two of us are headed to Georgia to be with the rest of our family. If I showed up in Georgia without him, they'd probably stone me to death! We've stuck together so far throughout this ordeal. It doesn't make sense for us to be separated now. If I can't go, he can't go!"

I guess she saw that I was adamant, so she didn't push the issue any further. She finally said, "Well, I'll have to see if there is a place that can take in both of you."

CHAPTER 13

Sabbath
A Place of Rest

Tuesday, September 6, 2005

Daddy and I spent a total of two-and a-half days at Camp Williams before our visit came to an abrupt end. Tuesday afternoon I was going back and forth throughout the military base, mingling with the other evacuees and running errands just as I had been doing for the previous days. As I approached the barracks, I saw Daddy and his belongings being loaded into a van. I ran up to the van and asked, "Daddy, where are you going?"

A tall, slender, middle aged gentleman, wearing tinted eyeglasses and a big smile stepped from behind the vehicle. He grasped my hand tightly and while shaking it he said, "Hi, you must be Cheryl, Emile's daughter. My name is Willie McMillan. Nurse Amy sent me here to take you and your father to our facility. I own the Friendly Village Nursing Home. That's where we're taking your father. We'll take good care of him while he's there."

Then Nurse Amy emerged from the barracks. When she saw me she said, "Oh Cheryl, there you are. I found a nursing home that will accommodate you and your father. We'll wait for you while you pack your bags."

I thought to myself, *she was serious. She wasn't joking. She actually took the time to find a place that would take in both of us! Wow!* I went inside and started packing, which took only five minutes. Then I came out, got into the van with Daddy, and we were on our way.

It was a 45 minute drive from Camp Williams to the Friendly Village Nursing Home in metro Salt Lake City, Utah. As we traveled, I had a tourist's view of the winding roads that hugged the picturesque mountainous landscape. It was a very soothing ride, almost therapeutic.

When we arrived, we were warmly greeted and welcomed by the facility's staff and medical personnel. Mr. Donald, the van driver, unloaded our bags and escorted us in. He was a short, sturdy man, approaching his golden years. He actually reminded me of Fred Mertz, from the *I Love Lucy Show* that aired in the late 1950's. First we met Stephanie, his wife, who was also the head nurse. She was tall, with dark hair that was styled in a short cut. She was a very talkative person and she made sure that all of Daddy's medical needs were taken care of during our stay. Then we met Elaine McMillan, Mr. Willie's wife and co-owner of the nursing home. She was also rather tall with blonde hair, very professional, very business-like. They took us in. We filled out the paperwork and got my Daddy settled in.

The nursing home, which housed about 28 clients, was a well-kept, rather pleasant facility, with a peaceful atmosphere. The entrance consisted of a Plexiglas sliding door. In the front of the building at ground level was a very spacious dining room and lounging area, which contained a 42" TV screen, a couple of lounge chairs and a sofa. As we exited the dining area through the double doors, we entered a long hallway, with a kitchen on one side and the nurse's station on the other. On both sides were the patients' rooms, two patients per room, set up sort of like a hospital. All of the offices were upstairs.

After getting Daddy settled in, they took me downstairs to a very spacious – but empty-four room apartment. The only furnishings were a bathtub, some empty cabinets and the kitchen sink. They told me this is where I'll be staying – after they furnished it. I was told that exactly one year ago a fire broke out in the apartment and it was totally destroyed, although there was no loss of life. They just finished renovating it and I was the first person to live there since the renovation. **I kid you not! Within 8 hours of my arrival to the nursing home I was living in a fully furnished apartment –rent free!** They went out and bought all new furniture and appliances and had it installed by nightfall! I had a 35" television with cable, a bed, lamp, clock, sofa, dining set, dishwasher, refrigerator, washing machine, dryer, towels, sheets, blanket, and pillows. What more could I ask for? All the people at the Friendly Village Nursing Home treated Daddy and me royally. We lacked nothing!

Wednesday, September 7, 2005

I noticed there were several husband-wife teams that worked at the facility. There were two geriatric workers, Mr. Lloyd and his wife, Leslie, who cared for the patients. They waited on my Daddy hand and foot and treated him like a king. They washed his clothes, changed his bedding, kept him clean, and made sure he got his meals on time. There was Roselyn, the head cook, who saw to it that all the meals were properly planned and that everyone's special diet was taken into consideration. Her husband was Mr. Joseph, the grounds keeper and repairman. They also lived in the downstairs apartment complex next door to me.

And, of course, there was the secretary, Mary Ann, who kept me laughing. She was my unofficial psychotherapist.

During the day I'd go to her office to make phone calls to my family members in preparation to go to Georgia. After I got off the phone and she took care of her workload, we'd talk for a while. Every morning she'd ask me, "Did you get a good night's sleep?" I couldn't give her a positive answer because I was still having nightmares about rising floodwater and helicopters flying overhead. It was as if anything that reminded me of the hurricane – the sound of dripping water or aircraft flying overhead – would trigger the entire scenario of New Orleans and my body would automatically react. I came to the conclusion that maybe the nightmares were just my subconscious mind dispelling all the bad memories of the event. The experience also affected me in a way that I was unaware of. During the past ten days I'd lost a significant amount of weight, about ten pounds or so. I could tell because my clothes were fitting me very loosely.

Thursday, September 8, 2005

One morning, as I was sitting in Mary Ann's office, she told me of an experience that she had when she was a young girl. When she was about four or five years old, she got up one morning to pour herself a glass of milk. She wanted to be very careful to not spill the milk in order to prove that she was a big girl. She got the milk out of the refrigerator, got a glass, pulled up a chair and stood on it so she could reach the tabletop. As she started pouring, an earthquake began. The table slid from one end of the kitchen to the other and back as little Mary Ann tried aimlessly to make the milk go into the glass. She cried desperately as she saw the milk spill all over the floor. Her mother soon rushed through the kitchen door, worried about her daughter's reaction to the earthquake. Mary Ann immediately tried to defend herself by saying, "Mommy, I didn't mean to spill the milk all over the floor on purpose! When I tried to pour it, the table kept moving, honest!" Her mother burst into laughter, and so did I when I heard that story! It was just what I needed to make my day.

Friday, September 9, 2005

When I wasn't in Mary Ann's office I would walk up and down the neighborhood and explore my new surroundings. Salt Lake City, unlike New Orleans, is full of hills and I enjoyed walking up and down them. As I walked, I made several observations about the neighborhood. Their streets were liter-free. There was a high Hispanic population in the area. There were many small businesses, or "mom & pop shops" like barber shops, guitar stores, motorcycle shops, cleaners, auto-repair shops, etc. The land was very spacious and people did not have to live on top of each other like we did in New Orleans. I also filled my time by going on outings with some of the residents from the nursing home. The employers provided off site activities for their residents such as trips to the library, shopping, bowling and movies. I went to two of these activities with the residents.

Although I was living a carefree life and everything was going very well in Utah, I was getting homesick and anxious to get to Georgia to be with the rest of my family. Thus, my family members and I started making a very diligent effort to find a means for us to get from Utah to Georgia. Initially, we were told that a certain airline was offering free transportation to hurricane evacuees so they could travel and be with their families.

But when we investigated this news, no one in that airline company seemed to have any knowledge of this. *DUH!* Then we were told that FEMA was providing vouchers for hurricane victims to get across the country to their families via bus. However, it was unrealistic for Daddy to take a bus ride that was over 24 hours long. It would be too stressful for him.

Finally, my youngest sister, Miriam, and her husband, Rodney, came up with the finances to purchase plane tickets for us to get from Salt Lake City to Birmingham, Alabama. There was no airline in Salt Lake City that had a direct connection to Atlanta, Georgia that costs under $500 for the two of us. This was the closest that we could get between the two cities for the price that we could afford. Someone would just have to pick us up from Birmingham and drive us back to Atlanta. Our family members loaned us the money until we could get on our feet again and pay them back. But at least we were finally on our way home!

CHAPTER 14

Our Desired Haven

Saturday, September 10, 2005

Daddy and I woke up early Saturday morning, eagerly anticipating our journey home. We had already packed the night before so all we had to do was say our "good-byes" to the staff and be on our way. Our plane left at ten that morning. We had a layover in Chicago for about 1 ½ hours, where we made the connecting flight, then flew to Birmingham, Alabama. As soon as we landed, which was about 6:40 p.m., some of our family members were already waiting to pick us up. The drive home took about three hours but we talked about the perils of the hurricane in New Orleans and our future in Georgia, so the ride didn't seem that long. Before we knew it, we were at my sister's house where everyone else was waiting for us. We finally reached our desired haven! It was about 10 p.m. by then and as soon as we came in everyone was begging us to tell the story of how in the world we made it through Hurricane Katrina. Daddy and I didn't even bother to unpack. Instead, we all sat around the kitchen table, turned on the camcorder, and I began sharing this story – the story that you've just read.

I could say that this is THE END of our story. But it really isn't. It is actually A NEW BEGINNING! This story continues because I have yet to embark upon the pages of my life which have already been written by the hand of God.

CHAPTER 15

Recovering All

I Samuel 30:18, 19
So David recovered all that the Amalekites
had carried away and David rescued his two wives.
And nothing of theirs was lacking, either small or great,
sons or daughters, spoil or anything
which they had taken away from them;
David recovered all!

During the first week of October, I had the opportunity to go back to New Orleans. Even after five weeks, the city was still a ghost town. Many streets were still littered with debris. Standing water still remained in certain parts of the city. Some of the bridges were still closed and the lower ninth ward still had not yet reopened to its residents. A relentless, unquenchable stench still lingered over the entire metro area. As we drove through the city, we decided that once we got to the house, we'd grab whatever we could as quickly as possible and get out of there!

You may be wondering if we were able to salvage any of our belongings from our home in New Orleans. Do you remember earlier in this book I stated that before we left the house I put all of our valued belongings on the top shelves and elevated places in the house? Well, it paid off! When we returned to assess the damage to our home and salvage whatever we could, we were able to get the most important things out – irreplaceable items that our family valued like photos, a few books, some music, personal possessions, etc. However, the house itself, like most of the houses in New Orleans, suffered major structural damage to the roof, walls and floors. All of the furniture and appliances were lost, and because of the toxic mold that had set in, the entire house needed to be gutted out.

I am ecstatic to report, however, that there was no loss of life within our entire extended family, nor among any of our relatives who lived in the metro New Orleans area. HALLELUJAH! We had a significant loss of property, but we all got out safely! Although we are scattered across the southeast now, we are all still alive and safe! We still stay in touch with each other and that is a testimony of the goodness of God!

Due to the hurricane, we've been forced to make some abrupt and major changes in our lives, but most of them have been very beneficial. My dad finally got sufficient care at home during the day, **which was next to impossible when we were living in New Orleans!** Many doors of opportunity have opened up to me and I can fulfill my life's dreams – like writing this book, teaching, and traveling. Regretfully, Hurricane Katrina was a disaster to many, but for my family and me, God turned this disaster into a MEGA blessing!

Romans 8:28

And we know that all things work together for the good to those who love God, to those who are the called according to His purpose.

Author, Cheryl Hawkins

About the Author

Cheryl K. Hawkins was born in the wee hours of the morning on Thursday, November 19, 1959 to the union of Emile and Meriam Hawkins and is the oldest of five children. She grew up in the Church of God in Christ and gave her heart to Jesus at age 16. She also embarked upon the music ministry by playing the piano for the youth choir of her church that same year.

Cheryl graduated from Oral Roberts University in 1982 with a Bachelor of Science Degree in Telecommunications. She later attended graduate school and obtained a Master's Degree in Education from the University of New Orleans in 1992. She has been an elementary school teacher for over twenty years. Cheryl has taught numerous Bible studies to inner city youth down through the years and has worked in many summer camps for disadvantaged children. She was a member of Light City Church where she served as a musician and songwriter for almost twenty years. She grew up in New Orleans, Louisiana, but now resides in suburban Atlanta, Georgia with the rest of her family members. Cheryl is currently a member of the East/West Worship and Conference Center, which is pastored by Bishop H. Alan Mushegan.

1994 Thanksgiving family gathering
From left to right;
My youngest sister, Miriam,Yolanda, Michele, Cheryl, my
mother, Meriam, whom we also called "Muh," my dad,
Emile Sr., and my brother, Emile Jr.

Cheryl and her siblings at their 2008 New Year's gathering.
Left to right; Emile Jr., Yolanda, Miriam, Cheryl and
Michele.

Here are my parents after forty years of marriage.
Daddy lived for exactly one year and six months after
relocating to Georgia. We had his funeral on April 7, 2007,
which was the date of his 72nd birthday.

CPSIA information can be obtained at www.ICGtesting.com
Printed in the USA
LVOW11s0710251114

415414LV00001B/52/P

9 781606 474419